MY FIRST
GARDEN
B·O·O·K

ANGELA WILKES

ALFRED A. KNOPF · NEW YORK

DK

A Dorling Kindersley Book

For Rose

Design Mathewson Bull
Photography Dave King
Editor Helen Drew
Production Marguerite Fenn
Managing Editor Jane Yorke
Art Director Roger Priddy

This is a Borzoi Book published by Alfred A. Knopf, Inc.

First American edition, 1992

2 4 6 8 10 9 7 5 3 1

Library of Congress Cataloging-in Publication Data
Wilkes, Angela.
    My first garden book / by Angela Wilkes.
        p. cm.
    Summary: Features simple gardening projects from collecting
seeds to growing a miniature desert garden.
    ISBN 0-679-81412-4 (trade) – ISBN 0-679-91412-9 (lib. bdg.)
    1. Gardening–Juvenile literature. [1. Gardening.] I. Title.
SB457.W55 1992
635–dc20   90-40332

Phototypeset by Setting Studio, Newcastle
Color reproduction by Colourscan, Singapore
Printed and bound in Italy by L.E.G.O.

Dorling Kinderley would like to thank Jonathan Buckley,
Mandy Earey, Richard Gilbert, and June King for their help
in producing this book.

Illustrations by Brian Delf

CONTENTS

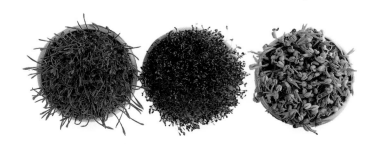

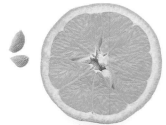

Gardening By Pictures

Growing things is easy and fun, and you do not need a garden!
My First Garden Book shows you how to grow flowers, herbs,
fruit, and vegetables on windowsills, balconies, and patios.
Step-by-step photographs show you exactly what to do, and
there are life-size photographs of the finished projects. On the
opposite page is a list of things to read before you start,
and below are the points to look for in each project.

How to use this book

The things you need
The plants and supplies for
each project are shown life-
size, to help you check that
you have everything.

Gardener's tools
These illustrated checklists
show you which pieces of
equipment to have ready
before you start a project.

Step by step
Step-by-step photographs
and clear instructions
show you what to do at
each stage of the project.

Window Garden

With a window box you can
look out on to a mass of flowers
without having to go outside.
Choose flowers in one or two
colors, or go for a riot of bright
colors. Look for plants with
interesting leaves and for
trailing plants to go at the front
of the window box. Here
you can see what to do.
The final result is
over the page.

GARDENER'S TOOLS

Trowel
Scissors
Watering can
Plant food
Plant sprayer

Bellflower

Impatiens

You will need
*Small plants
(two or three
of each sort)*

Marguerite

*Sand-based potting
soil*

*Clay pellets,
gravel, or ashes*

*A window box with drainage
holes in the bottom*

Pansy

Drip tray

What to do

1 Fill the bottom of the window
box with a layer of clay pellets
about 1 inch deep to keep the soil
from becoming soggy.

2 Half fill the window box with
potting soil. If the soil is very
dry, water it before you start
planting anything.

3 Keeping the plants in their
pots, arrange where to put
them. Tall plants should go at the
back and trailing ones at the front.

4 One at a time, take each plant
out of its pot and gently
loosen its roots by pulling them
free from potting soil.

5 Dig a small hole. Gently put
the first plant in, making sure
its roots have enough room. Press
down the soil around the plant.

6 Plant the other plants. Fill in
the gaps between them with
soil and press it down firmly,
leaving space for watering.

40

41

Things to remember

1 Read the instructions before you start, to make sure you have everything you need.

2 Check when to plant different things and which growing conditions are best for them.

3 Put on an apron or old shirt and roll up your sleeves before you start.

4 Cover your worktable with newspaper before you start each project.

5 When you have finished working with your garden, clean your tools, clean up any mess, and put everything away.

6 Water and check your seeds and plants regularly once you have planted them, and watch them as they grow.

7 Be patient. Do not give up if things do not start to grow right away.

8 Some plants for a project may not be available where you live. If so, ask someone at your garden store to recommend a replacement.

The final results
Life-size pictures show you what the finished projects look like, making it easy for you to copy them.

Aftercare
Many of the projects have step-by-step instructions showing you how to care for the things you have planted.

Information
The finished projects often have notes telling you more about particular plants.

GARDEN IN BLOOM

And here is the finished window box! You can copy this one or try your own plant arrangements. Ask an adult to help you move the full window box, because it is heavy and must sit safely on a strong window ledge. If the window ledge slopes, wedge pieces of wood under the front of the box to keep it level.

Watering
Water the window box enough to keep the soil slightly moist. It will need watering every day in warm weather.

Deadheading
The plants in the window box will keep their flowers longer if you regularly pick or snip off any dead flower heads.

Feeding
Once every six weeks or so, "feed" the plants by adding a little liquid plant food to the water in your watering can.

Pest control
The simplest way to get rid of insects on the plants is to spray them with warm water with liquid soap added to it.

New plants
If one of the plants in the window box dies, carefully dig it up. Plant another plant in its place, pressing the soil firmly around it.

The finished window box

MARGUERITE
This is a small plant that produces pretty daisylike flowers throughout the summer.

IMPATIENS
Easy to look after, these plants have flat-faced, brightly colored flowers. They will stay in flower for most of the summer.

PANSY
We used two apricot-colored pansies and two purple ones. Keep pansies well watered and deadhead them often.

BELLFLOWER (Campanula)
This trailing variety of bellflower can also be grown as an indoor plant. It blooms from late summer to early winter.

42

43

GARDEN KIT

Here are some of the tools and other things that you will need to start gardening. They are usually shown in the "gardener's tools" boxes in the book. Gather together the things for your kit, and you will be ready to start planting and watching things grow!

Potting soil. This is light soil with plant food added to it. There are different types of potting soil: some for seeds and cuttings and others for larger plants

Gravel (or clay pellets), to keep the holes in flowerpots from getting blocked

Small watering can

Liquid plant food, to replace the minerals in soil that plants use up

Scissors

Seed trays with drainage holes in the bottom

Drip trays to match the different sizes of your flowerpots

Plant sprayer

6

Marker pen, for labeling things

Teaspoon,
for moving seedlings

Trowel

Small fork

Garden twine
or string

Garden
sticks, for
supporting droopy plants

Flowerpots in different sizes with
drainage holes in the bottom

Small envelopes, for collecting seeds

Ties, for holding plants to sticks

Plant labels

Plastic bags, for covering
flowerpots after planting seeds

SEED SEARCH

You can easily buy flower seeds, but it is more interesting to collect them yourself. Seeds come in a wide variety of shapes and sizes, depending on how different plants scatter them. You can gather flower seeds throughout the summer and collect tree seeds in the autumn. When collecting things, only take what you need and make sure you leave plenty of specimens behind. Here are some of the interesting types of seed that you may find.

Collecting seeds

Look for seeds once a flower's petals have died and a seed head has formed. The seeds are ripe when they are brown. Cut off the seed head and shake the seeds into a paper bag. Put the seeds in a small envelope, seal and label it, and keep it in a cool, dark place.

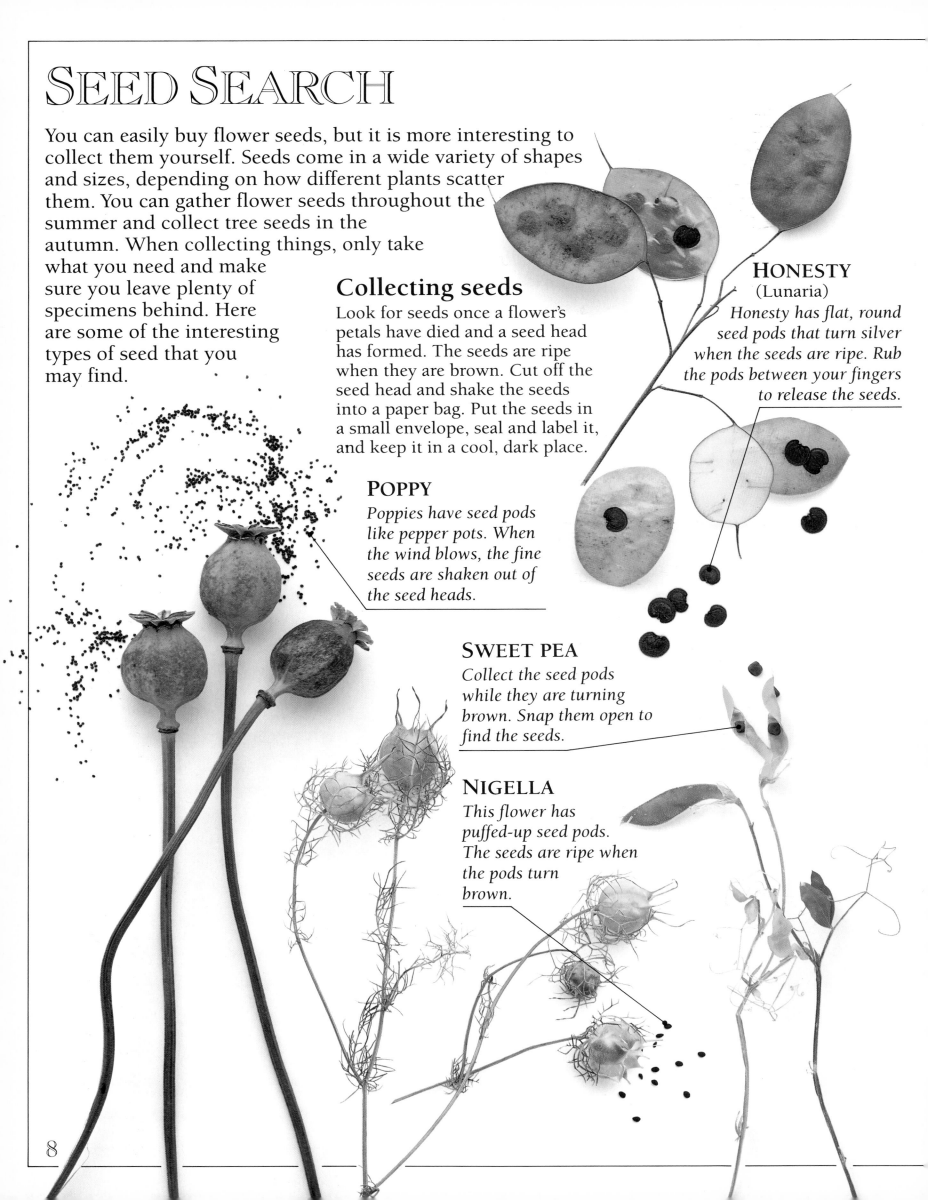

HONESTY
(Lunaria)
Honesty has flat, round seed pods that turn silver when the seeds are ripe. Rub the pods between your fingers to release the seeds.

POPPY
Poppies have seed pods like pepper pots. When the wind blows, the fine seeds are shaken out of the seed heads.

SWEET PEA
Collect the seed pods while they are turning brown. Snap them open to find the seeds.

NIGELLA
This flower has puffed-up seed pods. The seeds are ripe when the pods turn brown.

8

Tree seeds

It is best to look for tree seeds early in the autumn, before the birds and animals have removed them. Store tree seeds in a cool, dark place until the end of the winter, then plant them.

PLANE TREE
The seeds are encased in unusual "bobbles."

MAPLE
Each set of "wings" carries two seeds.

ACORNS
These are the seeds of the oak tree.

HORSE CHESTNUTS
The shiny seeds are carried in prickly cases.

SUNFLOWER
The striped seeds are packed together in unusual patterns on the massive flower heads.

HOLLYHOCK
Pick the seed heads from the tall stems once the flowers have died.

MARIGOLD
Marigolds have tight clusters of crescent-shaped seeds that turn brown as they ripen.

PLANTING SEEDS

Plant flower seeds indoors in early spring, and they will be big enough to plant outside once the weather is warm. You can grow most *annuals* and *biennials** from seed. Read the seed packages to find out when to plant seeds, the growing conditions they need, and when to water them. If you have gathered the seeds and aren't sure of the growing conditions, check with a gardening store.

You will need

*Seed-and-cutting soil***

Ties for plastic bags

Plant labels

Acorns

Nasturtium seeds

Sunflower seeds

Poppy seeds

Plastic bags

GARDENER'S TOOLS

Seed trays

Flowerpots and drip trays

Trowel

Watering can

Pen (for labels)

What to do

1 Fill the flowerpots and seed trays with soil to about ½ inch from the top of the pot. Water the soil lightly.

2 Planting big seeds. Push each one about ½ inch deep into the soil. Label each pot with the name of the seed planted in it.

* Annuals live for one year. Biennials live for two years, but usually only flower the second year.

** Special potting soil for young plants.

3 Plant small seeds in seed trays. Sprinkle the seeds onto the soil. Cover them with a thin layer of soil. Label the tray.

4 Tie plastic bags over the flowerpots and seed trays and put them in a warm, dark place.† Check the seeds every day.

5 As soon as shoots appear, take off the plastic bags and move the seeds into the light. Water the soil enough to keep it damp.

†Such as a closet.

From seed to plant

Some of the easiest flowers to grow are nasturtiums. Here you can see how a seedling develops. This plant stayed in one pot, but seedlings planted in seed trays will need to be carefully dug up and moved to separate pots or into the garden once they are big enough.

1

You can see the nasturtium's first two leaves.

2

The seedling grows fast. The first two leaves grow bigger. The stem shoots up between the leaves, and more leaves appear. The young plant needs a lot of light.

3

4

Buds appear, then the nasturtium starts to flower. As it is a climbing plant, you should tie it to a garden stick when it grows bigger. The plant will twine around the stick.

11

SALAD GARDEN

You don't always need flowerpots and potting soil to grow things. You can grow all sorts of tasty, crunchy things to add to salads on nothing more than cotton soaked in water. Try sprouting different seeds, beans, and grains, and you can harvest your own mini-crops of vitamin-packed salad sprouts in about a week. The seeds will sprout all year round, and you can grow them on a windowsill or in any well-lighted place indoors. A health food store is a good place to buy the things you need.

You will need

Different seeds:

Wheat grains

Alfalfa seeds

Mustard seeds

Mung beans

Cress seeds

Cotton

GARDENER'S TOOLS

Shallow dishes

Ties

Plastic bags

Bowl

Strainer

Glass jars

Pen

Labels

Plant sprayer

What to do

1 Rinse large beans and grains in a strainer under a cold tap. Put each kind in a jar of warm water to soak for 12 hours, then rinse them.

2 Dip pieces of cotton in cold water, then gently squeeze most of the water out. Line the dishes with the damp cotton.

3 Sprinkle a tablespoonful of one type of bean or grain over the cotton in each bowl. Label each one to say what is in it.

4 Tie plastic bags loosely over the bowls to keep the seeds moist. Put the bowls in a warm, dark place. Check them every day.

5 As soon as the seeds sprout, take off the plastic bags and move them to a light place. Spray them with water every day.

The sprouting seeds

Most of the seeds, beans, and grains will have started to sprout in two to three days. They will be ready to pick after five to seven days, when they are still young and tender. Snip them off the cotton and sprinkle them on salads or add them to sandwiches.

MUNG BEANS

These are the bean sprouts used in Chinese cooking. Pick them when they are still pale and have no leaves.

ALFALFA

This grows very quickly and looks like cress with smaller leaves.

WHEAT

This looks like young grass. Snip it and sprinkle it on salads or add it to your pet's food.

BULBS

Many of the prettiest spring flowers grow from bulbs and are easy to raise indoors. Buy bulbs in autumn and plant them right away to flower the next spring. Plant small bulbs in small pots and grow only the same plants in any one pot, so that they all flower at the same time.

All bulbs must be put in a cool, dark place for a while to form the strong roots that will let them bloom well. Turn the page to see a stunning array of flowers grown from bulbs.

You will need
Different bulbs:

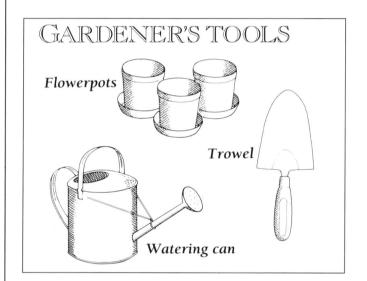

GARDENER'S TOOLS

Flowerpots

Trowel

Watering can

Gravel or clay pellets

Hyacinths

Dwarf tulips

Daffodils

Planting bulbs

1 Shovel a little gravel or some clay pellets into the bottom of your flowerpots or containers to keep the soil from becoming soggy.

2 Half fill the flowerpots with potting soil. You may want to add special bulb fertilizer to the soil.

3 Arrange big bulbs close together with their pointed ends up. Add more soil. Let the bulbs poke out of the soil.

Potting soil

Narcissi

Grape hyacinths

Crocuses

Miniature irises

What is a bulb?

Here the bulb of a hyacinth in flower has been cut in half so that you can see what is inside it.

Food supply

A bulb is like an onion inside. It is a kind of underground food store. The plant rests for most of the year, then uses the food in the bulb to grow a stem, leaves, and flowers.

Roots

Bulbs have to grow strong roots before they can be brought into the light.

4 Arrange small bulbs with the pointed ends up. Add enough soil to cover them and fill the pot to about 1 inch below the rim.

5 Water the pots, then put them in a cool, dark place for 8 to 12 weeks. Check the soil now and then to make sure it is moist.

Turn the page to see what to do next.

Spring Flowers

When the bulbs have shoots about 1 inch tall, move the flowerpots into the light, but keep them in a cool place. Most bulbs will flower four to five months after planting. They will flower best in a cool room. When the flowers have died, cut off the dead flower heads and let the leaves dry up, then plant the bulbs outside if you can, since they will not flower indoors again. The beautifully colored flowers shown here all bloom in early spring.

DWARF DAFFODIL

"Tête-à-tête" is a tiny golden daffodil with swept-back petals. It is a member of the narcissus family of bulbs.

CHIONODOXA

Commonly known as "glory-of-the-snow." Has starry blue flowers with white eyes.

CROCUS

One of the first spring flowers, it has funnel-shaped white, purple, or yellow flowers. Grows from a corm.*

SCILLA

This tiny plant has small, bright blue, bell-shaped flowers.

16   **A stem that grows under the surface of the soil.*

PUSCHKINIA

This tiny rock garden plant has spikes of star-shaped white or pale blue flowers.

HYACINTH

Hyacinths have heavy spikes of sweetly scented flowers, which may need supporting with garden sticks. Try growing hyacinths in water in glass jars so that you can watch the roots grow.

WATERLILY TULIP

A dwarf tulip which has white flowers with red and yellow centers. Like other lily-flowered tulips, the flowers open out flat in the sun.

17

HANGING BASKETS

A hanging basket is one of the prettiest mini-gardens you can make, and you can hang it anywhere. We used spring flowers in blues and yellows for our basket. For a summer basket, look for fuchsias, geraniums, lobelia, and impatiens. Turn the page for the finished basket.

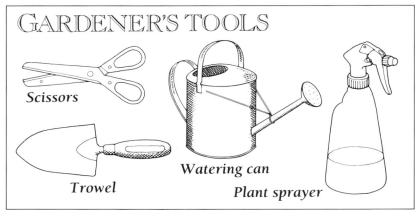
You will need

Lightweight potting soil

A wire basket with a chain handle

Sphagnum or peat moss

Pansies

Grape hyacinths

Plastic trash bag

Primulas or polyanthuses

Drumstick primula

Trailing variegated (two-color) ivy plants

Planting the basket

1 Line the inside of the wire basket with a thick layer of sphagnum moss. You should not be able to see any light through it.

2 Cut a piece of the trash bag big enough to line the inside of the basket. Lay it over the moss and cut off any plastic edges that show.

3 Wrap each ivy plant in a small piece of plastic shaped into a cone. The narrow end of the cone should be around the leaves.

19

Garden In A Basket

Here is the finished basket, overflowing with spring flowers. A hanging basket is very heavy when it is full, so ask an adult to hang it up for you and check that it is fastened securely. Hang it in a place where you can see the plants properly, and make sure that it is low enough for you to water easily.

Planting the basket (continued)

4 Make holes in the plastic bag. Thread the cone-wrapped leaves of the ivy plants through the holes. Pull the plastic cones away.

5 Thread a few pansies through the base of the basket in the same way, then half fill the basket with potting soil.

GRAPE HYACINTHS
These pretty spring flowers grow from bulbs, but you can buy them as plants too.

SPHAGNUM OR PEAT MOSS

CHAIN

PRIMULA

DRUMSTICK PRIMULA
There are many different kinds of primula. They all flower in early to mid spring.

6 Arrange and plant the rest of the plants in the basket. Fill the gaps between the plants with soil and water them well.

Watering

Water and spray the basket just enough to keep the soil damp. Baskets need watering once or twice a day in hot weather.

Deadheading

PANSIES
These are winter-flowering pansies. They will flower throughout the winter and spring, as long as you deadhead them regularly.

VARIEGATED IVY
Trailing ivy plants are useful for hanging baskets as they provide greenery and trail prettily around the bottom of the basket.

The plants in the basket will last longer if you regularly snip off any dead flower heads or leaves. Replace any plants that die.

DESERT GARDEN

Buy some small succulents and you can create a miniature desert in your own home. Succulents are plants that can survive without much moisture because they store water in their fleshy leaves or stems. Choose non-prickly plants with contrasting shapes, colors, and textures, and try out different arrangements in a shallow container or tray. Turn the page to see a desert garden.

You will need
Small succulents:

Sedum sieboldii

GARDENER'S TOOLS

Small spoon

Watering can

Trowel

Scissors

Wart plant
(Haworthia attenuata)

Gravel or coarse pebbles

Sand-based potting soil

Grit or coarse sand

Shallow container or deep tray

Hen-and-
chickens
(Echeveria)

What to do

1 Put a thin layer of gravel in the bottom of the container. Cover with potting soil until the container is half full.

2 Keeping the plants in their pots, try out different arrangements to see where you want to plant them.

*Flaming
Katy*
(Kalanchoe
blossfeldiana)

3 Carefully remove the plants from their pots, one at a time, and plant them. Fill in the gaps between them with more soil.

4 Gently spoon grit or coarse sand over the surface of the soil, then water lightly to settle the soil and plants.

*Sedum**

Jade plant
(Crassula
argentea)

Elephant bush
(Portulacaria afra)

*Sedum**

*There are more than
200 different types of sedum.

DESERT IN MINIATURE

Succulents like a lot of light, so put the finished mini-desert in a brightly lit window. The plants have a rest period in winter, so water the garden less often then. If you can, put the desert garden outside in a sunny, sheltered spot during the warm summer months, as this helps the plants to grow stronger.

Watering

Water the desert garden only when the surface of the soil has dried out. Desert plants like to dry out and then be well watered.

Trimming

If any of the plants grow long and straggly "branches," cut them off with a small pair of scissors.

SEDUM

ELEPHANT BUSH
(Portulacaria afra)

SEDUM

WART PLANT
(Haworthia attenuata)

FLAMING KATY
This plant's bright flowers last a long time. Replace it when it has stopped flowering, as it will not flower again.

24

The finished garden

The miniature desert garden looks surprisingly green and fresh. To add interest to the garden, you could arrange decorative pebbles or shells around the plants.

JADE PLANT
(Crassula argentea)
This plant is also sometimes known as the money plant.

Replacing plants

HEN-AND-CHICKENS
(Echeveria)
The name comes from this plant family's habit of growing baby plants around the main plant.

1 If a plant grows too big, gently dig it up with a teaspoon and replant it in a flowerpot or container of its own.

SEDUM SIEBOLDII

2 Replace the big plant with a smaller one. Slide the new plant out of its pot, plant it, and firm the soil and sand around it.

25

STRAWBERRY FEAST

Gardening is not just about growing flowers or indoor plants; you can also grow many different things to eat. Try growing your own strawberry plant and watching how the berries actually develop. And you do not need much space – with a little care, you can grow scrumptious strawberries in a simple flowerpot. Here you can find out what to do, and on the next two pages you can see how the flowers and fruit grow.

Young strawberry plant or plants. You can buy these at garden centers from late spring onward.

GARDENER'S TOOLS

Trowel

Scissors

Watering can

You will need

Loam or sand-based potting soil

A flowerpot for each plant

Gravel or clay pellets

What to do

1 Put a layer of gravel about ½ inch deep in the bottom of the flowerpot to keep the soil from becoming soggy.

2 Shovel a little potting soil into the flowerpot, leaving plenty of space for the strawberry plant's roots.

Drip tray for each flowerpot

3 If the strawberry plant's roots are all curled up, gently untangle them with your fingers and shake them free of extra soil.

4 Lower the plant into the flowerpot so that its roots touch the potting soil and its crown* is just below the pot rim.

5 Fill the flowerpot almost to the top with soil, heaping it up to the base of the plant's leaves. Firm the soil down.

6 Give the plant a good watering. Check the potting soil regularly and water it enough to keep it slightly moist.

*The place where the roots join the stem.

FROM FLOWER TO FRUIT

While strawberries are woodland plants and grow well in the shade, the fruit will grow and ripen better if the plants are kept in a sunny place either indoors or outside. Water the soil often enough to keep it slightly moist. Then sit back, wait, and watch carefully as the flowers are transformed into perfect, delicious strawberries.

The growing plant

1 At first, the plant just grows more and bigger leaves. Then a stem grows and flower buds appear at the end of it.

From bud to flower

2 The buds open out into white flowers with yellowish-green centers. When the flower petals die and fall off, the centers of the flowers start to swell.

Flower bud protected by the green, cup-shaped calyx.

If the plant grows any runners, cut them off at the base. This helps the plant to grow better fruit.

Swelling center of flower

Bud

Flower

Green strawberry

Flower

Green strawberries

3 The plant is still flowering. The centers of the first flowers now look like small, hard, green strawberries. Keep the plant well watered while the fruit is forming.

The leaves are still growing

Unripe, green strawberries

The ripening fruit

4 The strawberries grow larger and heavier. As they ripen, they turn a creamy color, then become tinged with pink. Finally they turn red.

Ripe strawberry

Dying flower

Picking

Pick the strawberries when they are red, keeping the little green caps on.

29

Fruit Seeds

Every time you eat fruit, you throw away the seeds or pit in the middle, but have you ever thought of planting them instead? If you give the seeds the right conditions and are patient, you will be surprised at what will grow: many seeds produce handsome plants. The best time of year to plant seeds is in the spring. Here you can find out how to plant an avocado pit and see how it grows.

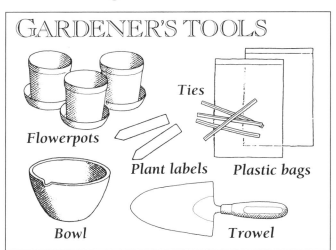

Gardener's Tools

Flowerpots

Ties

Plant labels

Plastic bags

Bowl

Trowel

Peach pit

Grape seeds

Orange or lemon seeds

You will need
Different seeds and pits:

Apple seeds

Potting soil or seed-and-cutting soil

Avocado pit

What to do

1 Soak big pits in water for 24 hours. Put some soil in a bowl and water it. Stir it well, then fill small pots with the soil.

2 Plant avocado pits pointed end up, sticking out of the soil. Plant seeds about ½ inch down in pots of soil.

3 Label each pot to say what is in it. Put each pot in a plastic bag and tie the bag at the top, then put the pots in a warm, dark place.

The growing plant

Check the flowerpots every day. As soon as you see a shoot, move the pot to a light place and take off the plastic bag. Water the young plant regularly, just enough to keep the soil moist, and watch it grow. Here you can see the first stages in the development of an avocado plant.

From pit to plant

Avocado pits take six to seven weeks to sprout. The pit splits, a root grows down into the soil, and a shoot emerges at the top.

New, young leaves

The stem grows quickly and the first leaves begin to open out.

Young side shoots

If the plant seems to be growing too tall, pinch off the growing shoot at the top. This encourages the plant to become bushier.

The first leaves soon grow quite large.

When the plant shows signs of growing too big for its pot, move it to a new, larger pot.

NEW PLANTS FROM OLD

Take cuttings from your houseplants in the spring and you can grow lots of new plants. A cutting is part of a plant that you cut off and plant so that it grows roots of its own. It may be a leaf, stem, or plantlet. Here you can see how to take three types of cuttings, and on the next page you can find out how to care for them.

You will need

Painted leaf begonia
These begonias have striking, colored, heart-shaped leaves and are ideal for leaf cuttings. You can also take leaf cuttings from African violets (Saintpaulias).

Potting soil or seed-and-cutting soil

Taking leaf cuttings

Tradescantia
It is easiest to take stem cuttings from tradescantia. Other good plants to take stem cuttings from are geraniums, mint, and coleus.

1 Cut a healthy-looking leaf and its stalk off a begonia or African violet. Plant the stalk in a pot of soil.

2 Water the soil to make it moist. Tie a plastic bag over the leaf and flowerpot and put it in a warm place out of the sun.

Taking stem cuttings

Spider plant
These trailing plants grow long runners with baby plantlets at the end, which you can pot to make new plants.

1 Cut a strong shoot about 2½ inches long off the tradescantia or other plant, just below a leaf. Trim off the bottom leaves.

2 Plant the cutting in a pot of soil. Or stand it in a glass of water so that you can watch it grow roots.*

Plantlets

1 The plantlets at the end of a spider plant's runners have roots. When the roots are ½ inch long, cut plantlets off the runners.

2 Trim the lower leaves off the plantlets, then plant them in small pots of moist soil, making sure the roots are covered.

GARDENER'S TOOLS

Trowel

Ties

Glass

Plant sprayer

Scissors

Flowerpots

Watering can

Plastic bags

* Once the cutting has grown roots, you should plant it in soil.
The plastic bag is optional for stem cuttings and plantlets.

33

FROM CUTTINGS TO PLANTS

Checking for growth

After a few weeks, take the bags off the pots and tug the cuttings gently. If the cuttings are rooted firmly in the soil, leave the bags off.

Watering

Keep an eye on the cuttings. Water them when the soil has dried out. It is best to put water in the drip trays, not in the soil.

Spraying

Gently spray the cuttings with water from time to time. This cleans the leaves and stems and stops them from drying out.

Here are some young plants growing from different types of cutting. The African violet and begonia started as leaf cuttings.

PAINTED LEAF BEGONIA

SPIDER PLANT
The spider plant was grown from a plantlet. You can pot plantlets from strawberry geraniums (Saxifraga stolonifera) in the same way.

AFRICAN VIOLET

Encouraging growth

If a baby plant is growing too tall and straggly, remove the tips of the growing shoots. This makes the plant become bushier.

Repotting

1 If roots are showing at the bottom of a plant's pot, you should repot the plant. Gently tip the plant out into your hand.

2 Plant it in a new pot, one size larger, filled with fresh new soil. Water the plant and put it in a shady place for about a week.

TRADESCANTIA
This tradescantia cutting has rooted in a glass of water. When the roots are 1-2 inches long, the cutting should be planted in a pot of soil.

AEONIUM
Some succulents grow small plants around their stem. Break these off and plant them in separate pots of soil.

ALUMINUM PLANT
This plant was grown from a stem cutting taken in the spring.

VEGETABLES IN POTS

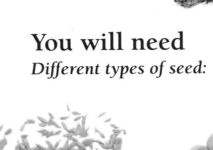

You don't need a garden to grow vegetables. You can grow small or dwarf varieties very successfully in flowerpots and other containers on a balcony, strong window ledge, or patio. Here you can see how to plant vegetables. Look at the backs of seed packages to find out when and where to plant them. Turn the page to see some vegetables growing!

GARDENER'S TOOLS

Trowel

Seed trays

Flowerpots

Watering can

Pen (for labels)

Plant sprayer

You will need
Different types of seed:

Lettuce

Dwarf pea

Dwarf runner bean

Beet

Radish

Zucchini

Plant food

What to do

1 Fill the seed trays and flowerpots with soil, and water the soil a little so that it is moist but not soaking wet.

2 Plant big seeds in flowerpots. Push each about ½ inch deep into the soil. Label the pots with the names of the seeds.

3 Plant small seeds in seed trays. Sprinkle them over the soil, then cover them with a thin layer of soil. Label them.

Clay pellets or gravel

Labels

Plastic bags and ties

Garden sticks

4 Spray the seed trays and flowerpots with water. Tie plastic bags over them and put them in a warm, dark place.*

5 As soon as shoots appear, take the plastic bags off the seeds and move them into the light. Spray the soil with water.

6 When the seedlings grow too big for their pots or trays, dig them up very carefully and plant them in separate flowerpots.

* Such as a closet.

VEGETABLES GALORE

Follow the instructions on the seed packages, and remember to water your vegetables often to keep the soil moist. Then watch them grow! Here you can follow the progress of a lettuce plant and a dwarf green bean plant.

LETTUCE

1

Tiny seedlings appear in the seed tray. The first true leaves are beginning to show.

2

One of the small lettuces has been moved to its own pot.

3

Pick the lettuce before its leaves open out too far.

DWARF GREEN BEAN PLANT

1

Remains of seed

First leaves

The stem grows quickly and the plant's first real leaves begin to open out from between the two halves of the old seed.

2

The leaves grow bigger...

3

...and bigger.

5

Young bean forming

Flowers

As the plant grows, twist the stem around a garden stick and tie it in place to give it support. Spray the flowers with water. This helps the beans to grow.

Tie

Garden stick

HARVESTING
The beans are tastiest when they are small. Pick them when they are about 4 inches long and snap easily when bent.

4

The plant is now growing very fast and young leaves are sprouting everywhere.

39

WINDOW GARDEN

With a window box you can look out on to a mass of flowers without having to go outside. Choose flowers in one or two colors, or go for a riot of bright colors. Look for plants with interesting leaves and for trailing plants to go at the front of the window box. Here you can see what to do. The final result is on the next page.

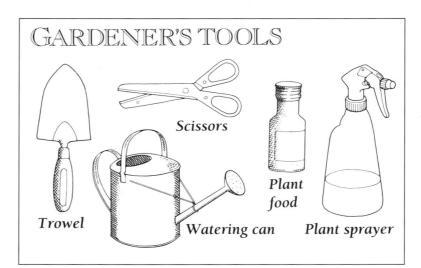

GARDENER'S TOOLS

Trowel

Scissors

Watering can

Plant food

Plant sprayer

Impatiens

You will need

Small plants
(two or three
of each kind)

Marguerite

Sand-based potting
soil

Clay pellets,
gravel, or ashes

A window box with drainage
holes in the bottom

What to do

Bellflower

Pansy

Drip tray

1 Fill the bottom of the window box with a layer of clay pellets about 1 inch deep to keep the soil from becoming soggy.

2 Half fill the window box with potting soil. If the soil is very dry, water it before you start planting anything.

3 Keeping the plants in their pots, arrange where to put them. Tall plants should go at the back and trailing ones at the front.

4 One at a time, take each plant out of its pot and gently loosen its roots by pulling them free from the potting soil.

5 Dig a small hole. Gently put the first plant in, making sure its roots have enough room. Press down the soil around the plant.

6 Plant the other plants. Fill in the gaps between them with soil and press it down firmly, leaving space for watering.

GARDEN IN BLOOM

And here is the finished window box! You can copy this one or try your own plant arrangements. Ask an adult to help you move the full window box because it is heavy and must sit safely on a strong window ledge. If the window ledge slopes, wedge pieces of wood under the front of the box to keep it level.

Watering

Water the window box enough to keep the soil slightly moist. It will need watering every day in warm weather.

Deadheading

The plants in the window box will keep their flowers longer if you regularly pick or snip off any dead flower heads.

The finished window box

MARGUERITE

This is a small plant that produces pretty daisylike flowers throughout the summer.

IMPATIENS

Easy to look after, these plants have flat-faced, brightly colored flowers. They will stay in flower for most of the summer.

Feeding

Once every six weeks or so, "feed" the plants by adding a little liquid plant food to the water in your watering can.

Pest control

The simplest way to get rid of insects on the plants is to spray them with warm water that has liquid soap added to it.

New plants

If one of the plants in the window box dies, carefully dig it up. Plant another plant in its place, pressing the soil firmly around it.

PANSY
We used two apricot-colored pansies and two purple ones. Keep pansies well watered and deadhead them often.

BELLFLOWER (Campanula)
This trailing variety of bellflower can also be grown as an indoor plant. It blooms from late summer to early winter.

HERB FEAST

For centuries people have grown herbs to flavor food, make medicines, and even to keep evil spirits away. Here and on the next three pages you can see how to re-create a traditional ornamental herb garden in a large container, full of useful kitchen herbs.

You will need
Small herb plants:

Oregano

GARDENER'S TOOLS

Trowel

Watering can

String

Scissors

Regular or flat-leaved parsley (you need eight small plants)

Lemon thyme

Gravel or clay pellets

Potting soil

Large square container

Planting the container

1 Fill the bottom of the container with a layer of gravel or clay pellets about 1 inch deep. This keeps the soil from becoming soggy.

2 Add soil to the container until it is about three quarters full. This allows plenty of space for planting the herbs.

3 Plant the feverfew in the center of the pot. Plant the parsley in two diagonal lines, crossing over the feverfew.

4 Plant the sage, rosemary, marjoram, and thyme in the triangular spaces between the lines of parsley.

5 Press the potting soil down firmly all around the plants. Add more soil if needed. Water the herbs well.

Rosemary

Purple sage

Feverfew

45

MINI KNOT GARDEN

Traditional knot gardens were divided into patterns by small hedge plants. In this knot garden, parsley is used to make a simple cross pattern and the other herbs give contrasting colors and textures. Here you can find out more about the herbs used.

PARSLEY

Parsley is one of the most useful kitchen herbs. It likes some shade and a lot of water. It only lasts for one summer, so you will need to replace it if you keep the knot garden longer.

ROSEMARY

An aromatic evergreen shrub with small blue flowers in spring. Rosemary grows best in a sunny, sheltered place. It grows tall, so keep it well trimmed.

GOLDEN FEVERFEW

A medicinal herb with aromatic golden-green leaves and pretty daisy-like flowers. Prefers a sunny position.

Trimming the herbs

Snip or pick the herbs often, especially the parsley, to help them grow bushy and to keep the shape of the knot garden.

PURPLE SAGE

One of many types of sage. A strongly scented evergreen plant with small, purplish flowers. Likes a sunny place.

LEMON THYME

One of many types of thyme. Dark green leaves with a lemon scent and tiny pink flowers in summer. Likes sun. Much loved by bees and butterflies.

BOUQUET GARNI

This is a small bunch or "bouquet" of fresh herbs used to add flavor to stews and casseroles.

Making a bouquet garni

Cut short sprigs of different herbs and tie them together in a small bunch with a piece of string, as shown.

OREGANO

Strongly flavored herb with pink or white flowers that attract bees. Likes sun. Perennial that needs to be cut back before winter.

Bushy Tops

When you buy vegetables in supermarkets, you think of them as something to eat and may never see what they look like when they are growing in the ground. Vegetables and fruit do not die when they are picked, and with a little patience you can grow surprisingly attractive plants from kitchen leftovers. Here you can find out how to grow bushy green plants from carrot and parsnip tops.

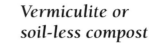

Vermiculite or soil-less compost

You will need

GARDENER'S TOOLS

Flowerpots

Knife

Plant sprayer

Carrots

Parsnips

NEW PLANTS

At the first sign of growth, put the flowerpots in a light place. Spray them with water to keep the vermiculite moist, and they will soon grow into strong, bushy plants. You can move them to larger pots of potting soil as they grow bigger, but they will not grow new carrots or parsnips.

What to do

Fill the flowerpots with vermiculite. Cut off the top of each vegetable.* Plant the tops on the vermiculite. Spray with water.

Put the flowerpots in a warm, dark place, such as a closet. Check them every day to make sure the vermiculite stays moist.

Be sure that an adult is present when you use the knife.